Who began their novel 'The past is a foreign country'? How did Orwell start *1984*? Who always has you smiling by the first comma? What opening line immortalizes the words 'One half of the world knows not how the other half lives'? Which author asks 'Is matchmaking at all in your line?' in his first sentence? How does *Gone With The Wind* start?

Find out this and much more in *First Lines*, a mine of pungent quotes from a wide range of novels, selected (from thousands upon thousands) by Gemma O'Connor, and delightfully caricatured by Wendy Shea.

From the risqué to the bizarre to the hilarious, all life is here.

D1642640

FIRST LINES

GEMMA O'CONNOR

ILLUSTRATIONS BY WENDY SHEA

Queen Anne Press/
Futura

A *Queen Anne Press / Futura* Book

© text Gemma O'Connor, 1985 & 1988
© illustrations Wolfhound Press, 1985 & 1988

This edition published in Great Britain in 1988 by
Queen Anne Press/Futura, A division of
Macdonald & Co. (Publishers) Ltd
3rd Floor
Greater London House
Hampstead Road
London NW1 7QX
A member of Maxwell Pergamon Publishing Corporation plc

First published in 1985 by Wolfhound Press,
68 Mountjoy Square, Dublin 1

ISBN 0 7088 42194

Reproduced, printed and bound in Great Britain by
Hazell Watson & Viney Limited
Member of BPCC plc
Aylesbury, Bucks, England

CONTENTS

For John, of course.

You and I, my good friend, have often deliberated on the difficulty of writing such a dedication as might gratify the self-complacency of a patron, without exposing the author to ridicule or censure of the public; and I think we generally agreed that the task was altogether impracticable.

To my silent friends.

O'Connor, Gemma. *First Lines*
Smollett, Tobias (1721-71) *The Adventures of Count Fathom (dedication)*
Mahaffy, John Pentland (1839-1919) *Principles of the Art of Conversation (dedication)*

INTRODUCTION

For the constant reader browsing at random, choosing his leisure reading, the opening lines are often what make him read on or slip the volume back on the shelf.

I started collecting first lines about five or six years ago. The idea of forming an anthology of the best, the most apt, and the most amusing soon occurred to me. As the interest grew and the pile of cards on which they were noted increased, it became apparent that though many were of intrinsic interest, most were not. Ask anyone to quote his favourite opening line and more likely than not the same ones are mentioned: Jane Austen, Tolstoy, Dickens and depending where you're from, Joyce. Was that, I wondered, because so few opening lines are memorable? That so few writers so precisely condense into the curtain-raiser the nub of the book? Some never manage a good one, and some, like Dickens, only a few in a vast body of work. James Stephens, especially in his short stories, does it every time and Saki has you smiling by the first comma. Did they and those like them not proceed until the first line was perfect — biting the end of the pen in the agonies of creativity and then hardly matching the splendour of that first punch with what followed? Well, there's always Jane Austen to disprove that.

A lot of famous names will be seen to be missing from this collection and for that I am sorry. Many writers start with a date or with proper or place names, this of course commands the attention of the reader but wasn't always what was required for my purpose. Although I began by looking for general observation rather than specific introductions, I sometimes went back to lines, rejected but half-remembered, to link the narrative.

This is a frivolous collection intended rather to entertain than instruct. To distract and amuse. It is an affectionate sidelong glance at the books that have given me great pleasure over the years, many of which are from my own shelves, since too often the piquancy of the opening lines has been enough to send me careering, bankrupt, out of the bookshop. I hope that the unfamiliar will prove an irresistible temptation to read on. Studying first lines has been an exercise in appreciation of the writer's technique, for it is in setting the scene that he becomes, briefly, a theatrical designer and the reader feels that first surge of excited anticipation. The great openers stand like beacons to the rest.

These first lines have been collected from works of prose, in English or in translation for the English-speaking reader. Verse has been excluded except as a link between one page and another, because the opening lines of a poem are more often good than not. (All the verse quotations are, in fact, openers.) Plays have not been included because first lines are usually stage directions (and in any case, I couldn't use *'exit, pursued by a bear!'*). Both poems and plays would and perhaps will, make books of their own.

Of course once the reader has become obsessed with first lines it takes no great leap of the imagination to turn to last lines. Sometimes the first and last lines match so beautifully that one can only assume more pen-biting on the part of the writer. Beryl Bainbridge, for example, in *The Dressmaker*:

Afterwards she went through into the little front room, the tape measure still dangling about her neck, and allowed herself a glass of port.

And in the dark she wiped the surface of the polished sideboard with the edge of her flowered pinny in case the bottle left a ring. . .

Still, it doesn't seem a general thing that having got an immortal first sentence the finale will equally oblige. In general it appears that writers are more interested in first than last, though there are some notable examples of the opposite.

It is one thing having a vast number of index cards

on which are noted an array of pithy, wise, funny, sad and downright odd sentences. Taken out of context, few stand as worth saying and some hardly make sense. What to do with them? At first I tried to arrange them into a kind of narrative using 'All the world's a stage' from *As You Like It*. But it soon became apparent that while it was easy to start it wasn't so easy to continue. However by now quite a lot of it was pleasingly arranged so I stuck with the device and broadened it to fit, loosely, into that fine blanket description: *La Comédie Humaine*. Soon the thing developed a life of its own and with pushing, pulling, rearranging, tearing-up, sorting-out and generally juggling around, it became apparent that something new was emerging from the material on hand: Further, that the dull as well as the quirky and wise could, when juxtaposed, change to something other. Lines discarded as being no use were retrieved from the wastepaper-basket; at the least they proved to be useful links and at best transformed the sense of the accompanying lines. Since theirs was the inspiration, I hope the Bard and Balzac will linger on, chuckling over the nonsense that has been made from deathless prose.

The urge to cheat was profound. Often the eye, slipping down the page, found the second paragraph far more alluring than the first and just the thing to pull the sense together. I was specially tempted to use the first line of the last chapter of *Jane Eyre*. Like many people I had remembered 'Reader, I married him' as the last line of the book and, having found that it was not, wanted to slot it into this volume. It is, it could be argued, a first line of sorts. But the temptation was firmly resisted and the original scheme firmly adhered to. Sometimes an opening line can incorporate a well known epigram or quotation from someone else (see Quiller-Couch). In two instances only I have slightly cheated, with apologies to David Piper and Simon Nowell-Smith; each has started a book with a quotation and these proved my undoing. My admiration for the appositeness of the lines quoted is my apology.

9

In the final reckoning only about one in twenty of the books I looked at yielded something that could be used within the structure imposed and rather fewer would number among the immortal opening lines that everyone knows and loves. One of the advantages of this exercise has been that I have sometimes come across writers long forgotten and some previously unknown to me whose first words so compelled my attention that there was no choice but to read on. At other times, a writer, well known in some other context, completely surprises one. How could anyone resist 'To write properly of asparagus, one needs a fine feathery pen'? From A. A. Milne known to me only for the enterprising *POOH*.

In trying to form a narrative from this random collection I hope to amuse the reader in an idle hour. It is a personal anthology and incomplete.

I should like to thank my friends who have suggested suitable opening lines to me — it has been an agreeable diversion though sometimes verging on the obsessive. Time to move on to last lines. In particular, special thanks to Michael Trevanion for some of the most amusing and apt.

My warmest thanks to my family whose encouragement and enthusiasm have made First Lines so enjoyable.

The Quarry
Oxford
August 1984

IN THE BEGINNING . . . .

'Goe, littel booke' and face thy fate.
Nor ever pause to explicate.
MICHAEL TREVANION.

Of Writers & Readers . . .

To study the changes of fashion in title pages one should begin at the actual beginning, and the beginning is to be found not on the first but on the last printed leaf of the early book.

The title of this work has not been chosen without the grave and solid deliberation, which matters of importance demand from the prudent.

The only apology which this work perhaps requires is with regard to the title, for otherwise it belongs to a class of publications, of which the value is so obvious as to admit of no question.

The title of this collection is like any other title; it could have been something else.

It is not my intention to detain the readers by expatiation on the variety or the importance of the subject, which I have undertook to treat; since the merit of the choice would serve to render the execution still more apparent, and still less excusable.

This title is not chosen to mystify my readers.

DeVinne, T. L. (1828-1914)   *Title Pages as seen by a Printer*
Scott, Walter (1771-1932)   *Waverley, or 'Tis Sixty Years Since*
Galt, John (1779-1839)   *The Bachelor's Wife*
O'Hara, John (1905-1970)   *Waiting for Winter (Introduction)*
Gibbon, Edward (1737-94)   *Decline & Fall of The Roman Empire*
Beerbohm, Max (1872-1956)   *Yet Again*

The only possible excuse for this book is that it is an answer to a challenge.

There are three difficulties in authorship; to write anything worth the publishing – to find honest men to publish it – and to get sensible men to read it.

Reader, I have put into thy hands what has been the diversion of my idle and heavy hours.

This book was compiled with a special purpose, and if it should not satisfy those for whom it was intended, no preface can save it.

It is very seldom that the preface of a work is read.

Except for a tendency to write articles about the Modern Girl and allow his side-whiskers to grow, there is nothing an author to-day has to guard himself against more carefully than the Saga Habit.

This book is largely concerned with Hobbits,

Reader, Loe here a well-meaning booke.

Chesterton, G. K. (1874-1936)   *Orthodoxy*
Colton, C. C. (1780-1832)   *Lacon or Many Things in a Few Words*

Locke, John (1632-1704)   *Essay on Human Understanding*
Bridges, Robert (1844-1930)   *The Spirit of Man*
Borrow, George (1803-81)   *The Bible in Spain*
Wodehouse, P. G. (1881-1975)   *Blandings Castle (Preface)*
Tolkien, J. R. (1892-1973)   *The Lord of the Rings*
Montaigne, Michel de (1533-92)   *The Essayes*

Among the many problems that beset the novelist, not the least weighty is the choice of the moment at which to begin his novel.

It is better, when practicable, to begin at the beginning of the episode.

Beginning this book (not as they say 'book' in our trade – they mean magazine), beginning this book, I should like if I may, I should like if I may (that is the way Sir Phoebus writes), I should then like to say: Goodbye to all my friends, my beautiful and lovely friends. And for why? Read on Reader, read on and work it out for yourself.

I believe that a well-known anecdote exists to the effect that a young writer, determined to make the commencement of his story forcible and original enough to catch the attention of the most blasé of editors, penned the first sentence:
" 'Hell!' said the Duchess"

I hate to read new books.

Alice was beginning to get very tired of sitting by her sister on the bank and of having nothing to do: once or twice she had peeped into the book her sister was reading, but it had no pictures or conversations in it, 'and what is the use of a book,' thought Alice, 'without pictures or conversations?'

Sackville-West, V. (1892-1962)   *The Edwardians*
Somerville & Ross (1858-1949) (1862-1915) *Dan Russel the Fox*
Smith, Stevie (1905-1971)   *Novel on Yellow Paper*
Christie, Agatha (1891-1976)   *The Murder on the Links*
Hazlitt, W. (1778-1830)   *On Reading Old Books*
Carroll, Lewis (1832-98)   *Alice's Adventures in Wonderland*

'Hell!' said the Duchess.

Idle reader, you can believe without any oath of mine that I would wish this book, as the child of my brain, to be the most beautiful, the liveliest and the cleverest imaginable.

The more books we read, the clearer it becomes that the true function of a writer is to produce a masterpiece and that no other task is of any consequence.

How very little does the amateur, dwelling at home at ease, comprehend the labours and perils of the author, and, when he smilingly skims the surface of a work of fiction, how little does he consider the hours of toil, consultation of authorities, researches in the Bodleian, correspondence with learned and illegible Germans – in a word, the vast scaffolding that was first built up and then knocked down, to while away an hour for him in a railway train.

The author ought to consider himself, not as a gentleman who gives a private or eleemosynary treat, but rather as one who keeps a public ordinary, at which all persons are welcome for their money.

It is the privilege of tale-tellers to open their story in an inn, the free rendezvous of all travellers, and where the humour of each displays itself, without ceremony or restraint.

Cervantes (1547-1616)   *Don Quixote (Prologue)*
Connolly, Cyril (1903-74)   *The Unquiet Grave*
Stevenson, R. L. (1850-94)   *The Wrong Box*
Fielding, Henry (1707-54)   *The History of Tom Jones*
Scott, Walter (1771-1832)   *Kenilworth*

Good wine needs no bush; but this story has to begin with an apology.

I am writing this for myself.

This vast theme, to the illustration of which the finest intellects and the most assiduous study have been for ages directed, can hardly be approached without temerity by an amateur, whose knowledge must be, necessarily, superficial and incomplete, compared with that possessed by professional students. As however, I have been invited . . . .

It is difficult for a man to speak long of himself without vanity; therefore I shall be short.

Let me tell you the story of my life.

Quiller-Couch, Sir Arthur (1863-1944)   *The Mayor of Troy*
O'Faolain, Sean (1900-   )   *And Again*
Grote, Mrs George   *On Art, Ancient & Modern*
Hume, David (1711-76)   *Life, Written by Himself*
Gorky, Maxim (1868-1936)   *A Confession*

And what is Life?

When God at first made man,
Having a glass of blessings standing by,
'Let us', said he, 'pour on him all we can:
Let the world's riches, which dispersed lie,
Contract into a span.'

GEORGE HERBERT The Pulley

And what is Life? an hour-glass on the run.
JOHN CLARE What is Life?

Once upon a time, and a very good time it was . . . .

It was the best of times, it was the worst of times, it was the age of wisdom, it was the age of foolishness, it was the epoch of belief, it was the epoch of incredulity, it was the season of light, it was the season of darkness, it was the spring of hope, it was the winter of despair, we had everything before us, we had nothing before us, we were all going direct to Heaven, we were all going direct the other way – in short, the period was so far like the present period, that some of its noisiest authorities insisted on its being received, for good or evil, in the superlative degree of comparison only.

Ours is essentially a tragic age, so we refuse to take it seriously.

All happy families resemble one another, each unhappy family is unhappy in its own way.

One of my friends observed to me in a letter, that many stories which are said to be *founded* on fact, have in reality been *foundered* on it.

They order, said I, this matter better in France.

Joyce, James (1882-1941)	*Portrait of the Artist as a Young Man*
Dickens, Charles (1812-70)	*A Tale of Two Cities*
Lawrence, D. H. (1885-1930)	*Lady Chatterley's Lover*
Tolstoy, Leo (1828-1910)	*Anna Karenina*
Southey, Robert (1774-1843)	*A Tale of Paraquay*
Sterne, Laurence (1713-68)	*A Sentimental Journey through France and Spain*

I wish either my father or my mother, or indeed both of them, as they were both equally bound to it, had minded what they were about when they begot me; had they duly considered how much depended upon what they were then doing; — that not only the production of a rational Being was concerned in it, but that possibly the happy formation and temperature of his body, perhaps his genius and the very cast of his mind; – and, for aught they knew to the contrary even the fortunes of his whole house might take their turn from the humours and dispositions which were then uppermost; – had they duly weighed and considered all this, and proceeded accordingly, - I am verily persuaded I should have made a quite different figure in the world, from that in which the reader is likely to see me.

My father, Blas of Santillane, after having carried arms many years for the service of the Spanish Monarchy, retired to the town in which he was born, where he chose a wife among the second-rate citizens, who, though she was no chicken, brought me into the world ten months after her marriage.

Sterne, Laurence (1713-68) *The Life & Opinions of Tristram Shandy*

Le Sage, Alain René (1668-1747) *The Adventures of Gil Blas de Santillane*

All Happy Families

My mother dandled me and sang,
'How young it is, how young!'

W. B. YEATS Song from the Player Queen

When that I was and a little tiny boy,
WILLIAM SHAKESPEARE Twelfth Night

When a man writes of himself or others the principle of truth should be the basis of his work.

I was once accused of being born with a silver spoon in my mouth, but I have no recollection of any such phenomenon.

My father was a plain and unpretending man,

Mother had a lot to say.

It is not that I half knew my mother. I knew half of her: the lower half – her lap, legs, feet, her hands and wrists as she bent forward.

Just occasionally you find yourself in an odd situation.

Comedy is a game played to throw reflections upon social life.

Haydon, Benjamin Robert (1786-1846)   *Autobiography*
Guinness, Bryan (1905-   )   *Dairy Not Kept*
De Quincey, Thomas (1785-1859)   *Autobiography*
Lavin, Mary (1912-   )   *Happiness*
O'Brien, Flann (1911-1966)   *The Hard Life*
Heyerdahl, Thor (1914-   )   *The Kon-Tiki Expedition*
Meredith, George (1828-1909)   *The Egoist*

In our family, as far as we were concerned, we were born and what happened before that is myth.

Father wanted a small family, but he also wanted an heir, and he had four daughters and two wives before he eventually had a son.

I was set down from the carrier's cart at the age of three and there with a sense of bewilderment and terror my life in the village began.

His baptismal register spoke of him pessimistically as John Henry, but he left that behind with the other maladies of infancy.

My father's family name being Pirrip, and my Christian name Philip, my infant tongue could make of both names nothing longer or more explicit than Pip, so I called myself Pip, and came to be called Pip.

Pritchett, V. S. (1900-1984)   *A Cab at the Door*
Bermant, Chaim   *The House of Women*
Lee, Laurie   *Cider with Rosie*
Saki (H. H. Munro 1870-1916)   *Adrian*
Dickens, Charles (1812-70)   *Great Expectations*

In my younger and more vulnerable years my father gave me some advice I've been turning over in my mind ever since.

As the streets that lead from the Strand to the Embankment are very narrow, it is better not to walk down them arm-in-arm.

Four and thirty years ago, Bob Ainslie and I were coming up Infirmary Street from the High School, our heads together, and our arms intertwisted, as only lovers and boys know how, or why.

Buck did not read the newspapers, or he would have known that trouble was brewing.

'You look worried, dear,' said Eleanor.

'Sent down for indecent behaviour, eh?' said Paul Pennyfeather's guardian.

All he knew was this: that after listening to his paunchy, bearded, shrewd father for a time; after looking at his mother troubled in her wisdom; after feeling in his sister's eyes a keen hostility, he would arise and leave the house, knowing they were all wrong.

A scandal is an unpleasant business anywhere, especially in a village.

Fitzgerald, F Scott (1896-1940)	*The Great Gatsby*
Woolf, Virginia (1882-1941)	*The Voyage Out*
Brown, Dr. John (1810-1882)	*Rab & His Friends*
London, Jack (1876-1916)	*The Call of the Wild*
Saki (H. H. Munro 1870-1916)	*Fur*
Waugh, Evelyn (1903-1966)	*Decline and Fall*
Byrne, Donn (1889-1928)	*Brother Saul*
Birmingham, George (1865-1950)	*A Public Scandal*

Learning

Alack! 'tis melancholy theme to think
How Learning doth in rugged states abide.

THOMAS HOOD The Irish Schoolmaster

... *died of drinking ink.*

Poets of all ages and of all denominations are unanimous in assuring us that there was once a period on this grey earth known as the Golden Age.

It is pleasant to be transferred from an office where one is afraid of a sergeant-major into an office where one can intimidate generals, and perhaps that is why history is so attractive to the more timid amongst us.

I am a schoolmaster by profession, or was.

It is a trite but true observation that examples work more forcibly on the mind than precepts: and if this be just in what is obvious and blameable, it is more strongly so in what is amiable and praiseworthy.

The first date in English History is 55 B.C., in which year Julius Caesar (The *memorable* Roman Emperor) landed like all other successful invaders of these islands, at Thanet.

The Government of France, in the days before the Revolution, was described by someone as a despotism tempered by epigram.

In 1747 the only son of Victor de Riqueti, Marquis de Mirabeau, died of drinking ink.

Gallia est omnis divisa in partes tres.

Benson, E. F. (1867-1940)   *Dodo*
Forster, E. M. (1879-1970)   *The Consolations of History*
DuMaurier, Daphne (1907-   )   *Not After Midnight*
Fielding, Henry (1707-54)   *Joseph Andrews*
Sellar, W. C. (1898-1951) and   *1066 And All That*
Yeatman, R. J. (1898-1968)
Birmingham, George (1865-1950)   *Ships and Sealing Wax*
Welch, Oliver   *Mirabeau*
Caesar, Julius (102-44 B.C.)   *De Bello Gallico*

From the two principal parts of our nature, Reason and Passion, have proceeded two kinds of learning, mathematical and dogmatical.

The education bestowed on Flora Poste by her parents had been too expensive, athletic and prolonged: and when they died within a few weeks of one another during the annual epidemic of the influenza or Spanish Plague which occurred in her twentieth year, she was discovered to possess every art and grace save that of earning her own living.

There are some characters that seem formed by nature to take delight in struggling with opposition, and whose most agreeable hours are passed in storms of their own creating.

Good sense is, of all things among men, the most equally distributed; and everyone thinks himself so abundantly provided with it, that those even who are the most difficult to satisfy in everything else, do not usually desire a larger amount of this quality than they already possess.

The two rarest things to be met with are good sense and good nature.

Hobbes, Thomas (1588-1679) *The Elements of Law, Natural & Politic*
Gibbons, Stella (1902-   )   *Cold Comfort Farm*
Goldsmith, Oliver (1730-74) *Life of Lord Bolingbroke*
Descartes, René (1596-1650) *Discourse on the Method of Rightly
                             Conducting the Reason and Seeking
                             the Truth in the Sciences*
Hazlitt, William (1778-1830) *On the Spirit of Obligations*

Of all the English athletic games, none, perhaps, presents so fine a scope for bringing into full and constant play the qualities both of the mind and body as that of cricket.

I don't know what will become of the boy: he's no good at school and no good at games.

When I was a young boy, or I was sick or in trouble, or had been beaten at school, I used to remember that on the day I was born my father had wanted to kill me.

I suppose the high-water mark of my youth in Columbus, Ohio, was the night the bed fell on my father.

Nyren, John (1764-1837)   *The Young Cricketer's Tutor*
Moore, Gerald (1899-)   *Am I Too Loud*
Renault, Mary (1905-83)   *The Last of the Wine*
Thurber, James (1894-1961)   *My Life and other Times*

In comparing modern with ancient manners, we are pleased to compliment ourselves upon the point of gallantry: a certain obsequiousness, or deferential respect, which we are supposed to pay to females as females.

The boys when they talked to the girls from Marcia Blaine School stood on the far side of their bicycles holding the handlebars, which established a protective fence of bicycle between the sexes, and the impression that at any moment the boys were likely to be away.

There is no doubt but youth is a fine thing.

Lamb, Charles (1775-1834)   *Modern Gallantry*
Spark, Muriel (1918-   )   *The Prime of Miss Jean Brodie*
O'Sullivan, Maurice (1904-1950) *Twenty Years A Growing*

The Phantoms of Hope

Queer are the ways of a man I know
THOMAS HARDY The Phantom Horseman

Ye who listen with credulity to the whispers of fancy, and pursue with eagerness the phantoms of hope; who expect that age will perform the promises of youth, and that the deficiencies of the present day will be supplied by the morrow; attend to the History of Rasselas Prince of Abissinia.

He, for there could be no doubt of his sex, though the fashion of the time did something to disguise it – was in the act of slicing at the head of the Moor which swung from the rafters.

Everybody has heard of the beautiful Countess of Cressett, who was one of the lights of this country at the time when crowned heads were running over Europe, crying out for charity's sake to be amused after their tiresome work of slaughter: and you know what a dread they have of moping.

All this happened a good many years ago.

The past is a foreign country: they do things differently there.

Johnson, Samuel (1709-84)   *The History of Rasselas*
Woolf, Virginia (1882-1941)   *Orlando, a Biography*
Meredith, George (1828-1909)   *The Amazing Marriage*
Maugham, W. Somerset (1874-1965)   *The Narrow Corner*
Hartley, L. P. (1895-1972)   *The Go-Between*

Reader, do you keep boys? Are you interested in them?

In one of the beautiful bays on the coast of Fairyland, a party of fairies was assembled on a lovely evening in July.

Neither her Gaudiness the Mistress of the Robes nor Her Dreaminess The Queen were feeling quite themselves.

'It is a pity that you have not my charm, Simon,' said Walter Challoner.

Unless one is wealthy there is no use in being a charming fellow.

From my youth upwards to the present moment, I never deserted a private friend, nor violated a public principle.

You're my friend.

Man is a born liar.

Pain, Barry (1864-1928)   *Playthings & Parodies, Boys*
Gatty, Mrs. Alfred (1807-73)   *The Fairy Godmothers &*
                                              Other Tales
Firbank, Ronald (1886-1926)   *The Flower beneath the Foot*
Compton-Burnett, Ivy (1892-1969) *A Heritage & Its History*
Wilde, Oscar (1854-1900)   *The Model Millionaire*
Parr, Dr. Samuel (1747-1825)   *Aphorisms, Opinions & Reflections*
Walpole, Hugh (1884-1941)   *Portrait of a Man with Red Hair*
O'Flaherty, Liam (1896-1984)   *Shame The Devil*

Of Man's First Disobedience and the Fruit
Of that Forbidden Tree . . .

JOHN MILTON Paradise Lost

Love righteousness, ye that be judges of the earth,

All true histories contain instruction; though, in some the treasure may be hard to find.

Can any thing, my good Sir, be more painful to a friendly mind than the necessity of communicating disagreeable intelligence?

Misery is manifold.

I shall not say why, and how, I became, at the age of fifteen, the mistress of the Earl of Craven.

Of course I have no right whatsoever to write down the truth about my life, involving as it naturally does the lives of so many other people, but I do so urged by a necessity of truth-telling, because there is no living soul who knows the complete truth; here, may be one who knows a section; and there, one who knows another section: but to the whole picture not one is initiated.

Thoroughly worldly people never understand even the world.

Apocrypha	*The Wisdom of Solomon I.i*
Brontë, Anne (1820-49)	*Agnes*
Burney, Fanny (1752-1840)	*Evelina*
Poe, Edgar Allan (1809-49)	*Bernice*
Wilson, Harriette (1789-1846)	*Memoirs of Herself & Others*
Nicolson, Nigel (1945-)	*Portrait of a Marriage*
Chesterton, G. K. (1874-1936)	*Orthodoxy*

Only a woman should write a woman's life.

In one of those seminaries devoted to female instruction, with which the environs of London abound, lived Miss Brideswell, whose sway within the limits of her own jurisdiction, was equal to that of the most potent monarch in the world, not excluding Napoleon himself.

Everything about her was extraordinary.

From the start she had known what she wanted, and proceeded, singleminded, with the force of a steam-engine, towards her goal.

First experiences should be short and intense.

There are two sorts of romantic: those who love and those who love the adventure of loving.

Pearson, Emma   *One Love in a Life*
Anon 19th Century   *Fatherless Fanny, The Memoirs of*
                                         a Mendicant
Blanch, Lesley (1907-   )   *Portrait of a Legend,*
                                         Isabelle Eberhardt
Blanch, Lesley (1907-   )   *A Two-Headed Profile, Isabel Burton*
Norwich, John Julius (1929-   )   *Venice, The Rise To Empire*
Blanch, Lesley (1907   )   *Matrimonial Theme & Variations,*
                                         Jane Digby

Matchmaking

When Farmer Oak smiled . . .

I was ever of the opinion, that the honest man who married and brought up a large family, did more than he who continued single and only talked of population.

It is a truth universally acknowledged, that a single man in possession of a good fortune, must be in need of a wife.

James Coshat-Prinkly was a young man who had always had a settled conviction that one of these days he would marry; up to the age of thirty-four he had done nothing to justify that conviction.

When Farmer Oak smiled, the corners of his mouth spread till they were within an unimportant distance of his ears, his eyes were reduced to chinks, and diverging wrinkles appeared around them, extending upon his countenance like rays in a rudimentary sketch of the rising sun.

There dwelt in Athens a young gentleman of great patrimonie, and of so comely a personage, that it was doubted whether he were more bound to Nature for the liniaments of his person, or to fortune for the increase of his possessions.

Is matchmaking at all in your line?

Goldsmith, Oliver (1730-74)	*The Vicar of Wakefield*	
Austen, Jane (1776-1817)	*Pride & Prejudice*	
Saki (H. H. Munro 1870-1916)	*Tea*	
Hardy, Thomas (1840-1928)	*Far From The Madding Crowd*	
Lyly, John (1554-1606)	*Euphues: The Anatomy of Wyt*	
Saki (H. H. Munro 1870-1916)	*The Forbidden Buzzards*	

Two ladies of good report . . .

In attempting a series of Narrative Poems on the Female Character, the Author's attention has been first directed to the less tender relations and less imperious duties of Woman.

In the days of high-waisted and muslin-gowned women, when the vast amount of soldiering going on in the country was a cause of much trembling to the sex, there lived in a village near the Wessex coast two ladies of good report, though unfortunately of limited means.

There was a woman who was beautiful, who started with all the advantages, yet she had no luck. She married for love; and the love turned to dust.

Lady Dolly ought to have been perfectly happy. She had everything that can constitute the joys of a woman of her epoch.

She thought that this marriage of all marriages would be an adventure.

There is a simplicity which comes from living too much in the world, as well as a simplicity which comes from living out of the world.

Mitford, Mary Russell (1787-1855)   *Narrative Poems on the Female Character*

Hardy, Thomas (1840-1928)   *The Trumpet-Major*

Lawrence, D. H. (1885-1930)   *The Rocking Horse Winner*
Ouida (Marie Louise de la Ramée 1839-1908)   *Moths*
Lawrence, D. H. (1895-1930)   *The Woman Who Rode Away*
Gibbons, Stella (1902-)   *Bassett*

The Widow Blacket

Girls are the young of women.

The widow Blacket, of Oxford is the largest female I ever had the pleasure of beholding.

Miss Brooke had that kind of beauty which seems to be thrown into relief by poor dress.

She was one of those attractive pretty girls born by a freak of fortune in a lower middle class family.

Was she beautiful or not beautiful? and what was the secret of form or expression which gave dynamic quality to her glance?

Years later, when she had gone and was no longer part of their lives, the thing they remembered about her was her smile.

Scarlet O'Hara was not beautiful, but men seldom realized it when caught by her charm.

Pain, Barry (1864-1928)	*Girls*
Lamb, Charles (1775-1834)	*Mrs. Leicester's School*
Eliot, George (1819-80)	*Middlemarch*
Maupassant, Guy de (1850-93)	*The Necklace*
Eliot, George (1819-80)	*Daniel Deronda*
DuMaurier, Daphne (1907-)	*Mary Ann*
Mitchell, Margaret (1900-49)	*Gone With The Wind*

Since the days of Adam, there has hardly been a mischief done in this world but a woman has been at the bottom of it.

The mystery of love is greater than the mystery of death.

For a long time I used to go to bed early.

Lolita, light of my life, fire of my loins. My sin, my soul . . . .

Men! Christ! And me. Me and men! What confusion.

Miss Braid, said: 'Men are . . . coarse!'

Dougal was in bed thinking about not being in bed.

I am the miserablest man living.

Nothing is true forever.

Thackeray, William Makepeace (1811-63) *The Luck of Barry Lyndon*
Wilde, Oscar (1854-1900) *Sebastian Melmoth*
Proust, Marcel (1871-1922) *Swann's Way*
Nabokov, Vladimir (1899-1977) *Lolita*
Hinde, Thomas (1926-) *Bird*
Brophy, Bridget (1929-) *The Finishing Touch*
Thompson, Eric *The Magic Roundabout*
Lamb, Charles (1775-1834) *The Last Peach*
Stephens, James (1882-1950) *The Triangle*

'Men are . . . coarse!'

Brightly dawns our wedding day . . .
W. S. GILBERT   A Merry Madrigal

I believe that in every decisive moment of our lives the spur to action comes from part of the memory where desire lies dozing awaiting the call to arms.

First of all I wish to speak of my wife.

Waking this morning out of my sleep on a sudden I did with my elbow hit my wife a great blow over her face and nose which waked her with pain at which I was sorry.

Stop crying, anyway, try to, that is.

Three passions, simple but overwhelmingly strong, have governed my life: longing for love, the search for knowledge, and unbearable pity for the suffering of mankind.

Lay with my wife at my Lord's lodgings where I have been these two nights, till 10 a clock with great pleasure talking; and then I rose.

'Love is the greatest of the passions', Miss Johnstone read, 'the first and the last.'

All nights should be so dark, all winters so warm.

O'Faolain, Sean (1900-   )   I Remember, I Remember
Moravia, Alberto (1907-   )   Conjugal Love
Pepys, Samuel (1633-1704)   Diary, Jan 1, 1661
O'Brien, Kate (1897-1974)   As Music and Splendor
Russell, Bertrand (1872-1970)   The Autobiography
Pepys, Samuel (1633-1703)   Diary, Jan 1, 1662
Hartley, L. P. (1894-1972)   Simonetta Perkins
Cruz Smith, Martin   Gorky Park

This is the story of what a woman's patience can endure and what a man's resolution can achieve.

Vanessa Pennington had a husband who was poor, with few extenuating circumstances, and an admirer who, though comfortably rich, was cumbered with a sense of humour.

The ordinary man's strongest point is his ignorance.

There was a woman who loved her husband, but she could not live with him.

Who was that woman?

Val Tuloch liked to look at her husband while he was reading, and not exactly chat – a word dangerously close to chatter – she liked to think of it rather, as speaking her thoughts.

Any fair-minded person must concede that words are not the tools of communication that, say, frowns and kisses are.

Marriage, said someone, is one long patience. It usually is not, but it ought to be.

Collins, Wilkie (1824-89)	The Woman In White
Saki (H. H. Munro 1870-1916)	Cross Currents
Pain, Barry (1864-1928)	In Lincoln's Inn Fields
Lawrence, D. H. (1885-1930)	Two Blue Birds
White, Patrick (1912-)	Riders in the Chariot
White, Patrick (1912-)	The Burnt Ones
Espy, Willard	The Game of Words
Bennett, Arnold (1867-1931)	The Night Visitor

Sir, Being ruined by the Inconstancy and Unkindness of a Lover, I hope, a True and Plain Relation of my Misfortune may be of Use and Warning to credulous maids, never to put too much trust in Deceitful Men . . .

The wrongs of woman, like the wrongs of the oppressed part of mankind, may be deemed necessary by their oppressors: but surely there are few, who will dare to advance before the improvement of the age, and grant that my sketches are not the abortion of a distempered fancy, or the strong delineations of a wounded heart.

Cur me querelis exanimas tuis? – in plain English, why do you deafen me with your croaking?

I was not born to command men.

There are various ways to mend a broken heart, but perhaps going to a learned conference is one of the more unusual.

The life of a scholar seldom abounds with adventure.

Swift, Jonathan (1667-1745)   *The Story of The Injured Lady*
Wollstonecraft, Mary (1759-97)   *The Wrongs of Woman, or Maria*
Scott, Walter (1771-1832)   *Redgauntlet*
Black, William (1841-98)   *Kilmeny*
Pym, Barbara (1913-80)   *No Fond Return of Love*
Goldsmith, Oliver (1730-74)   *The Life of Thomas Parnell*

Railways and Junctions

As, at a railway junction, men
Who came together, taking then
One train up, one down again...

ARTHUR HUGH CLOUGH Sir Itur

Other people enjoy themselves.

In my youth the suburbs were rather looked down on – I never quite knew why.

Along this particular stretch of line no express had ever passed.

Outside the station, people settled down again to being emotionally commonplace.

In the first place, Cranford is in possession of the Amazons; all the holders of houses, above a certain rent, are women.

A woman stood on her back step, arms folded, waiting.

There was no possibility of taking a walk that day.

Other people enjoy themselves, Mrs. Carter said.

'There's more to life up this end', Mrs. Poulter said.

Ah! you Ladies! Always on the spot when there's something happening.

Beerbohm, Max (1872-1956)   No. 2 The Pines
Huxley, Aldous (1894-1963)   Chrome Yellow
White, Patrick (1912-   )   The Living & The Dead
Gaskell, Mrs. (1810-65)   Cranford
Lessing, Doris (1919-   )   The Summer Before Dark
Brontë, Charlotte (1816-55) Jane Eyre
Greene, Graham (1904-   )   The Blue Film
White, Patrick (1912-   )   The Solid Mandala
Pym, Barbara (1913-1980)   Excellent Women

It has sometimes occurred to me that the great suits of armour we see in museums, the huge helmets that come down like extinguishers on the penny candles of modern humanity, the enormous cuirasses and gigantic iron gloves, were neither more or less than downright and deliberate cheats practised by the 'gents' of those days for the especial humbugging of us their remote posterity.

In some towns there are houses more depressing to the sight than the dimmest cloister, the most melancholy ruins, or the dreariest stretch of sandy waste.

Hillingdon Hall was one of those nice old-fashioned, patchy, up-stairs and down-stairs sort of houses.

'It is not a large house,' I said.

The double doors at the end of the ballroom were thrust open.

'Don't look now,' said John to his wife, 'but there are a couple of old girls two tables away who are trying to hypnotise me.'

Under certain circumstances there are few hours in life more agreeable than the hour dedicated to the ceremony known as afternoon tea.

Lever, Charles James (1806-72)   *Sir Jasper Carew*
Balzac, Honoré de (1799-1850)   *Eugenie Grandet*
Surtees, R. S. (1805-64)   *Hillingdon Hall*
Jerome K. Jerome (1859-1927)   *They And I*
Brophy, Brigid (1929-)   *The Snow Ball*
DuMaurier, Daphne (1907-)   *Don't Look Now*
James, Henry (1843-1916)   *The Portrait of a Lady*

Afternoon Tea.

The Bishop was feeling seasick.

Someone mentioned the sea.

We are off!

Fog everywhere, fog up the river, fog down the river, fog on the Essex marshes, fog on the Kentish Heights.

It was clearly going to be a bad crossing.

'How the wind is rising' said Rosamond, 'God help the poor people at sea tonight!'

After dinner we gathered on deck.

The Bishop was sitting in the stern of the boat.

The Bishop was feeling rather seasick.

It might have happened anywhere, at any time, and it could certainly have been a good deal worse.

The cabin-passenger wrote in his diary a parody of Descartes: 'I feel discomfort, therefore I am alive.'

I am, therefore, I think.

Lynch, Liam (1937-)	Shell, Sea Shell
Melville, Herman (1819-91)	Mardi, & a Voyage Thither
Dickens, Charles (1812-70)	Bleak House
Waugh, Evelyn (1903-66)	Vile Bodies
Edgeworth, Maria (1767-1849)	Patronage
Maupassant, Guy de (1850-93)	Fear
Lavin, Mary (1912-)	The Great Wave
Douglas, Norman (1868-1952)	South Wind
Howard, E. J. (1923-)	The Sea Change
Greene, Graham (1904-)	A Burnt Out Case
Banville, John (1945-)	Birchwood

Well Connected

Spurn not the nobly born
   With love affected,
Nor treat with virtuous scorn
   The well connected.

W. S. GILBERT Blue Blood

'Take my camel dear'

I had better let the cat out of the bag at once and record my opinion that the character of the English is essentially middle-class.

Throughout the latter part of his life, my Uncle Charles, having plenty of time to spare and little money, was a frequent guest of a wide range of more or less unwilling friends.

'Take my camel dear,' said Aunt Dot as she climbed down from this animal on her return from High Mass.

'Where have I seen that face before?' said a voice.

'Heavens' exclaimed the aunt of Clovis, 'here's someone I know bearing down on us, I can't remember his name, but he lunched with us once in Town.'

'So of course,' wrote Betty Flanders, pressing her heels rather deeper in the sand, 'there was nothing for it but to leave'.

Forster, E. M. (1879-1970)   *Notes on the English Character*
Balchin, Nigel (1908-70)   *Last Recollections of my*
                                       Uncle Charles
Macaulay, Rose (1881-1958)   *The Towers of Trebizond*
Wodehouse, P. G. (1881-1975)   *Boxing Final*
Saki, (H. H. Munro) (1870-1916)   *The Talking out of Tarrington*
Woolf, Virginia (1882-1941)   *Jacob's Room*

Of late years, an abundant shower of curates has fallen upon the north of England: they lie very thick on the hills; every parish has one or more of them: they are young enough to be very active, and ought to be doing a great deal of good.

I do not wish to speak of curates in the natural state, of curates in church.

The new curate seemed quite a nice young man, but what a pity it was that his combinations showed, tucked carelessly into his socks when he sat down.

He had a high nose. He looked at one over the collar, so to speak.

It was love at first sight, the first time Yosarian saw the chaplain he fell madly in love with him.

Many years ago it was the fashion to ridicule the idea of 'love at first sight', but those who think, not less than those who feel deeply, have always advocated its existence.

Brontë, Charlotte (1816-1855)   Shirley, A Tale
Pain, Barry (1864-1928)   Playthings and Parodies, Curates
Pym, Barbara (1913-1980)   Some Tame Gazelle
Stephens, James (1882-1950)   Three Heavy Husbands
Heller, Joseph (1923-)   Catch 22
Poe, Edgar Allan, (1809-1849)   The Spectacles

An abundant shower of curates

What true-bred city sportsman has not in his day put off the most urgent business, perhaps his marriage, or even the interment of his rib – that he might 'brave the morn' with that renowned pack, the Surrey subscription fox-hounds?

The Pytchley hounds have had a run. Io triumphe!

They were on their way.

Last night I dreamt I went to Manderlay again.

Ten more glorious days without horses!

'What do you think would happen', Colonel Theodore Roosevelt asked his son Kermit, 'if I shot an elephant in the balls?'

All my life I have felt a
great kinship with the
madman and the
criminal.

The mad cannot sin.

Surtees, R. S. (1805-64)   *Jorrocks' Jaunts and Jollities*
Whyte-Melville (1821-78)   *Holmby House*
Keating, H. R. F. (1926-)   *The Murder of the Maharajah*
DuMaurier, Daphne (1907-)   *Rebecca*
Murdoch, Iris (1919-)   *The Red and The Green*
Boyd, William (1952-)   *An Ice-Cream War*
Miller, Henry (1891-1980)   *The Brooklyn Bridge*
O'Faolain, Julia (1932-)   *Women In The Wall*

Since money is the fount of all modern adventure, the City of London, which holds more money to the square yard than any other place in the world, is the most romantic of cities.

It was a bright cold day in April and the clocks were striking 13.

Captain Crosbie came out of the bank with the pleased air of one who has cashed a cheque and has discovered that there is a little more in his account than he thought there was.

The possessive instinct never stands still.

The young man who, at the end of September 1924, dismounted from a taxicab in South Square, Westminster, was so unobtrusively American that his driver had some hesitation in asking for double his fare. The young man had no hesitation in refusing it.

The tourist is at the mercy of every kind of ruffian.

Bennett, Arnold (1867-1931)	*Teresa of Watling Street*
Orwell, George (1903-50)	*1984*
Christie, Agatha (1891-1976)	*They Came to Baghdad*
Galsworthy, John (1867-1933)	*The Forsyte Saga – In Chancery*
Galsworthy, John (1867-1933)	*The Forsyte Saga – A Modern Comedy*
O'Flaherty, Liam (1896-1984)	*A Tourists' Guide to Ireland*

Great Deeds & Noble Sorrows

'Say not the struggle nought availeth'
ARTHUR HUGH CLOUGH

. . . he had no intention of calling his mother-in-law a hippopotamus.

The season of strikes seemed to have run itself to a standstill.

When Reginald Iolanthe Perrin set out for work on the Thursday morning, he had no intention of calling his mother-in-law a hippopotamus.

He had really wanted to be a cheerful bum lying under a tree in a good climate writing poetry.

One day he chucked his job, put up his tools, told the boss he could do this and that, called hurroo to the boys, and sauntered out of the place with a great deal of dignity and one week's wages in cash.

Elmer Gantry was drunk.

He lifted the dustbin and looked out.

'The Bottoms' succeeded to 'Hell Row'.

If I am out of my mind, it's all right with me, thought Moses Herzog.

L'homme est né libre, et partout il est dans les fers. (Man is born free and is everywhere in chains)

Saki (H. H. Munro 1870-1916)   *The Unkindest Blow*
Nobbs, David   *The Fall & Rise of Reginald Perrin*
Porter, Katherine Anne (1890-   )   *That Tree, from Flowering Judas*
Stephens, James (1882-1950)   *Here Are Ladies*
Lewis, Sinclair (1885-1951)   *Elmer Gantry*
Milligan, Spike (1918-   )   *A Potboiling Dustbin of Bits*
Lawrence, D. H. (1885-1930)   *Sons and Lovers*
Bellow, Saul (1915-   )   *Herzog*
Rousseau, Jean-Jacques (1712-1778) *Du Contrat Social*

A paternal legislature, ever anxious, in its sentimental way, to keep women cribbed and coddled and ranked with children, decreed that all pit-workers shall leave their work at two o'clock on Saturday afternoons; thus spoiling the task of male workers (as these have often told me), and driving them, three hours earlier than usual, into the public house.

Complaints are to be heard everywhere about the growing dislike of work among English people.

Not a day passes over the earth but men and women of no great note do great deeds, speak great words, and suffer noble sorrows.

Below the belt all men are brothers.

The cat is the offspring of a cat and the dog of a dog, but butlers and lady's maids do not reproduce their kind. They have different duties.

One thing was certain, the white kitten had nothing to do with it – it was the black kitten's fault entirely.

One half the world knows not how the other half lives.

Munby, A. J. (1826-1910)   *Dorothy, (Preface)*
Birmingham, George (1865-1950) *Ships and Sealing Wax*
Reade, Charles (1814-84)   *The Cloister and the Hearth*
Miller, Henry (1891-1980)   *An Open Letter to Surrealists*
                                   Everywhere

Wells, H. G. (1866-1946)   *Chapter The First*
Carroll, Lewis (1832-98)   *Through The Looking Glass*
Lever, Charles (1806-72)   *Luttrell of Arran*

One half the world . . .

Querulous Age

We live in a querulous age; more, we live in an age which it is argued that to be happy is frivolous, and expecting to be happy positively childish.

The time which passes imperceptibly makes the same gradual change in habits, manners, and character, as in personal appearance.

Reaching the age of forty is a natural process that causes us much mental pain and gives us the opportunity to disturb our minds.

Every promise of the soul has innumerable fulfillments; each of its joys ripens into a new want.

Mr. Salteena was an elderly man of 42 and was fond of asking people to stay with him. He had quite a young girl staying with him of 17 named Ethel Monticue.

Quite ordinary people sometimes behave in a quite extraordinary way.

Levin, Bernard (1928-   )   *Enthusiasms*
Scott, Walter (1771-1832)   *The Abbott*
Wells, H. G. (1866-1946)   *The History of Mr. Polly*
Emerson, R. W. (1803-1882)   *Love*
Ashford, Daisy (1881-1972)   *The Young Visiters*
Plomer, William (1903-1973)   *Four Countries*

I have noticed that when someone asks for you on the telephone and, finding you out, leaves a message begging you to call him up the moment you come in, as it's important, the matter is often more important to him than to you.

Mr. Blingham, and may he fry in his own cooking-oil, was assistant treasurer of the Flaver-Saver company.

Fifty-five. Tallish – but stoutish. Dressed like the country gentleman which he was not and never would be.

He simply said my name.

He was one of those men who call ladies by their Christian names.

Call me Ishmael.

It has been common in recent years for people to speak of searching for their own identity.

Maugham, Somerset (1874-1965)	*Cakes and Ale*
Lewis, Sinclair (1885-1951)	*Kingsblood Royal*
Bennett, Arnold (1867-1931)	*Lord Raingo*
O'Brien, Edna (1930-)	*The Love Object*
Stephens, James (1882-1950)	*Three Women*
Melville, Herman (1819-91)	*Moby Dick*
Plomer, William (1903-73)	*The Autobiography*

To most men the past is never yesterday, or five minutes ago, but distant.

This is the year of my seventieth birthday, a fact that bewilders me.

The old gentleman condescended to accept the last cigar I had, and having lit it with my only match, he earnestly advised me never to smoke to excess, because this indulgence brought spots before the eyes, deteriorated the moral character, and was moreover, exceedingly expensive.

On the journey from London down to Sussex, Major Ronald Lucie-Browne was entrapped into conversation by an elderly gentleman, who lost no time in revealing that he had once been a Captain, and went on to relate that he was an expert in the science of firing a revolver.

It does a bullet no good to go fast; nor a man, if he is truly a man, no harm to go slow; for his glory is not at all in going, but in being.

And I certainly do enjoy listening to you gentlemen and getting your views.

Miller, Henry (1891-1980)   *Of Art and The Future*
Pritchett, V. S. (1900-   )   *Midnight Oil*
Stephens, James (1882-1950)   *There Is A Tavern In The Town*
Gibbons, Stella (1902-   )   *Matchmaker*
Ruskin, John (1819-1900)   *Selections from his Writings*
Lewis, Sinclair (1885-1951)   *The Man Who Knew Coolidge*

Tread softly and circumspectly in this funambulatory Track and narrow Path of Goodness: pursue virtue virtuously: leven not good Actions nor render Virtues disputable: stain not fair Acts with foul intentions: maim not uprightness by halting Concomitances, nor circumstantially deprave substantial Goodness.

What is moral and what is unmoral?

Fate intended me for a singularly fortunate man.

It was the afternoon of my eighty-first birthday, and I was in bed with my catamite when Ali announced that the Archbishop had come to see me.

Stately plump Buck Mulligan came from the stairhead, bearing a bowl of lather on which a mirror and razor lay crossed. A yellow dressing gown, ungirdled, was sustained gently behind him by the mild morning air, he held the bowl aloft and intoned:

Introibo ad Altare Dei

He was one who would have passed by the sphinx without seeing it.

Browne, Sir Thomas (1605-1682)   *Christian Morals*
Miller, Henry (1891-1980)   *The Immorality of Morality*
Jerome K. Jerome (1859-1927)   *Paul Kelver*
Burgess, Anthony (1917-   )   *Earthly Powers*
Joyce, James (1882-1941)   *Ulysses*
Stephens, James (1882-1950)   *The Blind Man*

It may be said, without offence to other Cities, of much greater consequence in the World, that our town of Dublin doth not want its due proportion of Folly, and Vice, both Native and Imported, we have the advantage to receive them last, and consequently after our happy manner to improve, and refine upon them.

It is a thing past all contesting, that, in the Reformation, there was a spirit of greater carnality among the champions of the cause, than among those who in later times so courageously, under the Lord, upheld the unspotted banners of the Covenant.

'Never,' wrote Reginald to his most darling friend, 'be a pioneer. It's the Early Christian that gets the fattest lion'.

'I maintain,' said Monsignor with a brisk air of aggressiveness and holding his pipe a moment from his mouth, 'I maintain that agnosticism is the only reasonable position in these matters'.

I hate people who have no notion of anything but generalities, forms, and creeds, and naked propositions.

Swift, Jonathan (1667-1745)   *The Intelligencer*
Galt, John (1779-1839)   *Ringan Gilhaise*
Saki (H. H. Munro 1870-1916)   *Reginald's Choir Treat*
Benson, R. H. (1871-1914)   *A Mirror of Shalott*
Hazlitt, William (1778-1830)   *On Reason & Imagination*

Though equal to all things unfit,
Too nice for a statesman,
too proud for a wit.

OLIVER GOLDSMITH Retaliation on Burke

It's the Early Christian . . .

That the author of the Religio Medici mounted on the airy stilts of abstraction, conversant about notional and conjectural essences; in whose categories of Being the possible took the upper hand of the actual; should have overlooked the impertinent individualities of such poor concretions as mankind, is not much to be admired.

The difficulty with a story like this is to know where to begin.

Now King David was old and stricken in years, and they covered him with clothes, but he gat no heat: wherefore his servants said unto him, let there be sought for my lord the king a young virgin, and let her stand before the king, and let her cherish him, and let her lie in thy bosom, that my lord the king may get heat.

Afterwards she went through into the little front room, the tape measure still dangling about her neck, and allowed herself a glass of port.

It is in the staging of her comedies that fate shows herself superior to mere human invention.

Lamb, Charles (1775-1834)   *Imperfect Sympathies*
Bentley, Nicolas (1907-78)   *The Tongue-tied Canary*
The Holy Bible   *The First Book of Kings* I. i-ii
Bainbridge, Beryl (1934-   )   *The Dressmaker*
Merriman, Henry Seton (1862-1903)   *In Kedar's Tents*

Afterwards . . .

There are few persons, even among the calmest thinkers, who have not occasionally been startled into a vague yet thrilling half-credence in the supernatural, by *coincidences* of so seemingly marvellous a character that, as *mere* coincidences, the intellect has never been able to receive them.

With a single drop of ink for a mirror, the Egyptian sorcerer undertakes to reveal to any chance comer far reaching visions of the past.

If I were drowning I couldn't reach out a hand to save myself, so unwilling am I to set myself up against fate.

The magician's experiment miscarried, because of the impossibility of getting pure and honest drugs in those days, and the result was that he transformed me into a cholera germ when he was trying to turn me into a bird.

A big grey gander it was.

I believe in the practise and philosophy of what we have agreed to call magic, in what I must call the evocation of spirits.

Poe, Edgar Allan (1809-49)   *The Mystery of Marie Roget*
Eliot, George (1819-80)   *Adam Bede*
Drabble, Margaret (1939-)   *The Waterfall*
Twain, Mark (1835-1910)   *Three Thousand Years Among
                                 the Microbes*

Macken, Walter (1915-67)   *Rain on the Wind*
Yeats, William Butler (1865-1939) *Magic, Ideas of Good & Evil*

The magician's experiment

Not Waving but Drowning

Nobody heard him, the dead man,
But still he lay moaning:
I was much further out than you thought
And not waving but drowning.
STEVIE SMITH Not Waving but Drowning

Certainly that Men were greedy of Life, who should desire to live when all the world were at an end; and he must needs be very impatient, who would repine at death in the societie of all things that suffer under it.

This, then, was the situation.

Marley was dead, to begin with: there is no doubt whatever about that.

When Brien O'Brien died, people said that it did not matter very much, because he would have died young in any case.

My father's funeral was full of priests.

I met my Aunt Augusta for the first time in more than half a century at my mother's funeral.

There were crimson roses on the bench; they looked like splashes of blood.

A funeral is never a cheerful ceremony.

Browne, Sir Thomas (1605-82)   *Religio Medici*
Howard, Elizabeth Jane (1923-   )   *The Long View*
Dickens, Charles (1812-70)   *A Christmas Carol*
Stephens, James (1882-1950)   *The Threepenny Piece*
Gordon, Mary (1949-   )   *Final Payments*
Greene, Graham (1904-   )   *Travels With My Aunt*
Sayers, Dorothy (1893-1957)   *Strong Poison*
Birmingham, George (1865-1950)   *Two Fools*

One may as well confess that, in the hands of a cunning literary craftsman, the theme of Murder as one of the Fine Arts attracts us more than we care to think about.

'Now listen carefully,' said the dying man,

Murder didn't mean much to Raven. It was just a new job.

Hale knew, before he had been in Brighton three hours, that they meant to murder him.

Someone must have been telling lies about Joseph K., for without having done anything wrong he was arrested one fine morning.

My True Name is so well known in the Records, or Registers at Newgate, and in the Old Baily, and there are some things of such Consequence still depending there, relating to my particular Conduct, that it is not to be expected I should set my Name, or the account of my Family to this work,

I have been here before, I said.

When he feels life to be hard, Mr Fortune is apt to argue that one of the chief causes of crime is the desire of the people to be good.

Hotson, Leslie (1897-   )   *The Adventure of a Single Rapier*
Benson, R. H. (1871-1914)   *The Dawn Of All*
Greene, Graham (1904-   )   *Gun For Sale*
Greene, Graham (1904-   )   *Brighton Rock*
Kafka, Franz (1883-1924)   *The Trial*
Defoe, Daniel (1660-1731)   *The History & Misfortunes*
                                  of The Famous Moll Flanders

Waugh, Evelyn (1903-1966)   *Brideshead Revisited*
Bailey, H. C. (1878-1961)   *Mr Fortune Wonders*

Important Places

Well, as Kavanagh said, we have lived
In important places.

SEAMUS HEANEY The Ministry of Fear

Everywhere in any country that owns remembered records there can be found in man's work, whether on stone or wood, or upon the living earth and water, vestiges of past happenings which lead the mind back along the trail of the past.

To atheists inadequately developed building sites; and often, alas, to Anglicans but visible symbols of disagreement with the incumbent: 'the man there is "too high", "too low", "too lazy", "too interfering"' – still they stand, the churches of England, their towers grey above billowy globes of elm trees, the red cross of St. George flying over their battlements, the Duplex Envelope System employed for collections, schoolmistress at the organ, incumbent in the chancel, scattered worshippers in the nave, Tortoise stove slowly consuming its ration as the familiar 17th century phrases come echoing down arcades of ancient stone.

There is a handsome parish church in the town of Woodstock.

It is a daily thing: a silent unvisited churchyard; bordering the garden of the parsonage; and holding a church whose age and interest spare our words; a few tombs fenced from their fellows, and marking generations of the family marked as great; others naming private lives that grew and waned by the spot which harbours their silence; and at some moment of its lying in sight an open grave with its mourners.

Gwynn, Stephen (1864-1950)   *The Famous Cities of Ireland*
Betjeman, John (1906-84)   *Guide to English Parish Churches*
Scott, Walter (1771-1832)   *Woodstock*
Compton-Burnett, Ivy (1892-1969) *Dolores*

To dwellers in a wood almost every species of tree has its voice as well as its feature.

In that pleasant district of merry England which is watered by the river Don, there extended in ancient times a forest, covering the greater part of the beautiful hills and valley which lie between Sheffield and the pleasant town of Doncaster.

The garden committee had met to discuss the earth; not the whole earth, the terrestrial globe, but a bit of it had been stolen from a garden in the square.

A wide plain, where the broadening Floss hurries on between its green banks to the sea, and the loving tide, rushing to meet it, checks its passage with an impetuous embrace.

'London is the most interesting, beautiful and wonderful city in the world to me, delicate in her incidental and multitudinous littleness, and stupendous in her pregnant totality . . . .'

I am a cockney among cockneys.

Hardy, Thomas (1840-1928)   *Under the Greenwood Tree*
Scott, Walter (1771-1832)   *Ivanhoe*
Godden, Rumer (1907-)   *An Episode of Sparrows*
Eliot, George (1819-80)   *The Mill On The Floss*
Piper, David (1918-)   *Guide To London, opening quotation from H. G. Wells*

Kingsley, Charles (1819-75)   *Alton Locke, Tailor and Poet*

The garden committee.

The ambiguous light of a December morning, peeping through the windows of the Holyhead mail, dispelled the soft visions of the four inside, who had slept or seemed to sleep, through the first seventy miles of the road, with as much comfort as may be supposed consistent with the jolting of the vehicle, and an occasional admonition to *Remember The Coachman*.

The people of France have made it no secret that those of England, as a general thing, are, to their perception, an inexpressive and speechless race, perpendicular and unsociable, unaddicted to enriching any bareness of contact with verbal wit or other embroidery.

I do not know where Ballymulligan is, and never knew anybody who did: once, asked the Mulligan in question, when that chieftain assumed a look of dignity so ferocious, and spoke of 'Saxon curiawsitee' in a tone of evident displeasure, that, as after all it can matter very little to me whereabouts lies the principality in question, I never pressed the inquiry any further.

Let not any one, about to travel to Greece, be induced by any thing under the absolute necessity to undertake the long week's journey from Naples to Brindisi or Otranto.

Palestine was a pleasant country if you came to it from Egypt.

Peacock, Thomas Love (1785-1866)	*Headlong Hall*
James, Henry (1843-1916)	*The Tragic Muse*
Thackeray, William Makepeace (1811-63)	*Mrs. Perkin's Ball*
Milnes, Richard Monckton (1809-85)	*Memorials of a Tour in Greece*
Jefferies, Ian	*Thirteen Days*

Beautiful Ireland!
Who will preach to thee?

LADY WILDE Who will show us any good?

When two countries, or sections of countries, stand geographically so related to one another that their union under a common government will conduce to the advantage of the stronger people, such countries will continue separate as long only as the country which desires to preserve its independence possesses a power of resistance so vigorous that the effort to overcome it is too exhausting to be permanently maintained.

Castes mark their children deeply; and as a caste the English Gentry resident in Ireland were pronounced.

It is the peculiar felicity and prudence of the people in this Kingdom, that whatever commodities and productions lie under the greatest discouragements from England, those are what they are sure to be most industrious in cultivating and spreading.

At the beginning of the year 1845 the state of Ireland was, as it has been for nearly seven hundred years, a source of grave anxiety to England.

Froude, James Anthony (1818-94)   *The English In Ireland*
Guedalla, Philip (1889-1944)   *The Duke of Wellington*
Swift, Jonathan (1667-1745)   *A Proposal for the Universal Use of Irish Manufacture in Clothes and Furniture of Houses etc.*

Woodham-Smith, Cecil (1896-1977)   *The Great Hunger*

Feudalism lasted long in Ireland.

It was one of those rare and perfect days which Ireland occasionally snatches from the impossible, and all the world seemed a glory of freshness and delight.

riverrun, past Eve and Adam's, from swerve of shore to bend of bay, brings us by commodious vicus of recirculation back to Howth Castle and environs.

Quaintly he came raiking out of Molesworth Street into Kildare Street, an old figure moidered by memories, making him turn himselfe into a merry mockery of all he had once held dear.

In any other city you would have noticed that fierce old man, but in Dublin he called for no more than a passing glance, so many are there who seem exiled kings.

'A quite legendary figure, a sort of stuffed waxwork from whose mouth a stream of coloured sentences, like winding rolls of green and pink paper, are forever issuing.'

Leslie, Shane (1885-1971) *Doomsland*
Crichton, F. E. *The Blind Side of the Heart*
Joyce, James (1882-1941) *Finnegans Wake*
Gogarty, Oliver St. J. (1878-1957) *As I was Going Down Sackville Street*
Byrne, Donn (1889-1928) *An Untitled Story*
Nowell-Smith, Simon (1909-) *The Legend of the Master – quotation from Hugh Walpole*

Exiled Kings

Time marched on Winkler

May I be permitted to chat a little, by way of recreation at the end of a somewhat toilsome and perhaps fruitless adventure?

In this age we read so much that we lay too great a burden on the imagination.

Well, time marched on Winkler, and, pursuing the policy of writing a book, then another book, then another book, then another book and so on, while simultaneously short stories and musical comedies kept fluttering out of me like bats out of a barn, I was doing rather well as scriveners go.

How much my life has changed, and yet how unchanged it has remained at bottom!

Now that I have completed my autobiography up to the present year I sometimes doubt whether it is right to publish it.

You will rejoice to hear that no disaster has accompanied the commencement of an enterprise which you have regarded with such evil forebodings.

Things had changed, but not utterly; and no terrible beauty had been born.

Browning, Robert (1812-89)   *The Agamemnon of Aeschylus*
AE (Russell, G. W. 1867-1935)   *Imaginations and Reveries*
Wodehouse, P. G. (1881-1975)   *Some Thoughts on Humourists Over Seventy*

Kafka, Franz (1883-1924)   *The Great Wall of China*
Rutherford, Mark (1831-1913)   *Autobiography*
Shelley, Mary (1797-1851)   *Frankenstein*
O'Casey, Sean (1884-1964)   *Innisfallen Fare Thee Well*

Like bats out of a barn

It is a common observation that few persons can be found who speak and write equally well.

There are a lot of critics in the world, just as there are a lot of authors too.

The making of an anthology of English prose is what must have occurred to many of its students, by way of pleasure to themselves, and of profit to other persons.

It is the fate of those who toil at the lower employments of life, to be rather driven by the fear of evil, than attracted by the prospect of good; to be exposed to censure, without hope of praise; to be disgraced by miscarriage, or punished for neglect, when success would have been without applause, and diligence reward. Among these unhappy mortals is the writer of dictionaries . . .

or, Anthologies? (G. O'C)

Hazlitt, William (1778-1830) On the Difference Between
                                Writing & Speaking
O'Casey, Sean (1884-1964)   The Green Crow
Pater, Walter (1839-94)   English Literature
Johnson, Samuel (1709-84)   A Dictionary of the English Language

ACKNOWLEDGEMENTS

The publisher gratefully acknowledges permission to quote first lines from copyright holders, authors or publishers as cited below. In a few instances we have been unable to contact the relevant copyright holder and would be grateful if they would contact the publisher.

Ashford, D.,*The Young Visiters* Chatto & Windus Ltd.; Bainbridge, B.,*The Dressmaker*, Duckworth; Balchin, N.,*Last Recollections of My Uncle Charles*, Collins; Banville, J.,*Birchwood*, Martin Secker & Warburg Ltd.; Beerbohm, M., *Yet Again, No. 2 The Pines*, Rupert Hart-Davis; Bellow, S., *Herzog*, Weidenfeld & Nicolson Ltd.; Bentley, N., *The Tongue-Tied Canary*, Curtis Brown; Bermant, C.,*The House of Women*, Weidenfeld & Nicolson Ltd.; Betjeman, J., *Guide to English Parish Churches*, Collins; Birmingham, G., *Ships and Sealing Wax, Two Fools*, A. P. Watt Ltd. and The Executors of the Estate of George Birmingham; Blanch, L., *Portrait of a Legend, Isabelle Eberhardt; Matrimonial Themes and Variations, Jane Digby; A Two-Headed Profile, Isabel Burton*, John Murray Ltd.; Boyd, W., *An Ice-Cream War*, Hamish Hamilton; Burgess, A., *Earthly Powers*, Hutchinson Ltd.; Chesterton, G. K., *Orthodoxy*, The Bodley Head; Christie, A., *The Murder on the Links*, The Bodley Head; *They Came to Baghdad*, Collins; Compton-Burnett, Ivy, *A Heritage and Its History, Dolores*, Victor Gollancz Ltd.; Douglas, N., *South Wind*, Chatto & Windus Ltd.; Drabble, M., *The Waterfall*, Weidenfeld & Nicolson Ltd.; du Maurier, D., *Not After Midnight, Don't Look Now, Mary Ann, Rebecca*, Curtis Brown Ltd. on behalf of Daphne du Maurier; Fitzgerald, F. S., *The Great Gatsby*, The Bodley Head; Forster, E. M. *Abinger Harvest*, Edward Arnold; Gibbons, S., *The Matchmaker, Bassett, Cold Comfort Farm*, Curtis Brown Ltd., London, on behalf of Stella Gibbons; Godden, R., *An Episode of Sparrows*, Macmillan; Gogarty, O., *As I Was Going Down Sackville Street*, Hutchinson Publishing Group Limited; Gordon, M., *Final Payments*, Literistic Ltd.; Greene, G., *A Gun for Sale, A Burnt-Out Case, Collected Stories, Travels With My Aunt, Brighton Rock*, William Heinemann Ltd. and The Bodley Head Ltd.; Guedalla, P., *The Duke of Wellington*, Hodder & Stoughton; Hartley, L. P., *Simonetta Perkins, The Go-Between*, Hamish Hamilton Ltd.; Heller, J., *Catch 22*, Jonathan Cape Ltd.; Heyerdahl, T., *The Kon-Tiki Expedition*, Allen & Unwin; Hinde, T., *Bird*, Hodder & Stoughton Ltd.; Howard, E. J., *The Long View, The Sea Change*, the author and Jonathan Cape Ltd.; Huxley, A., *Chrome Yellow*, Chatto & Windus Ltd.; Joyce, J., *Finnegans Wake*, The Society of Authors & Estate of James Joyce; *A Portrait of the Artist as a Young Man*, The Executors of the Estate of James Joyce, *Ulysses*, The Bodley Head; Keating, H. R. F., *The Murder of the Maharajah*, Collins; Lee, L., *Cider with Rosie*, The Hogarth Press Ltd.; Leslie, S., *Doomsland*, Lady Iris C. Leslie; Lessing, D., The Summer Before The Dark, the author and Jonathan Cape Ltd.; Lewis, S., *The Man Who Knew Coolidge, Elmer Gantry, Kingsblood Royal*, Jonathan Cape Ltd.; Macaulay, R., *The Towers of Trebizond*, Collins; Macken, W., *Rain on the Wind*, Macmillan; Maugham, W. S., *Cakes and Ale, The Narrow Corner*, The Executors of the Estate of W. Somerset Maugham; Moravia, A., *Conjugal Love*, Martin Secker & Warburg Ltd.; Miller, H., *Of Art and the Future, An Open Letter to Surrealists Everywhere, The Brooklyn Bridge, The Immorality of Morality*, Granda Publishing Ltd. and New Directions Publishing Corporation; Milligan, S., *A Potboiling Dustbin of Bits*, Michael Joseph; Mitchell, M., *Gone With The Wind*, Macmillan; Moore, G., *Am I Too Loud*, Hamish Hamilton; Murdoch, I., *The Red and the Green*, the author and Chatto & Windus; Nabokov, V., *Lolita*, Weidenfeld & Nicolson Ltd.; Nicolson, N., *Portrait of a Marriage*, Weïdenfeld & Nicolson Ltd.; Nobbs, D., *The Fall & Rise of Reginald Perrin*, Victor Gollancz Ltd.; Norwich, J. J.,*Venice, The Rise to Empire*, Penguin Books Ltd.; O'Brien, E., *The Love Object*, Jonathan Cape Ltd.; O'Brien, F., *The Hard Life*, Granada Publishing Limited; O'Casey, S., *The Green Crow, Inishfallen Fare Thee Well*, Macmillan; O'Faolain, J., *Women in the Wall*, Deborah Rogers Ltd. and Penguin

Books; O'Faolain, S., *And Again, I Remember, I Remember*, Constable; O'Hara, J., *Waiting for Winter*, Random House Inc.; Orwell, G., *1984*, the Estate of the the late Sonia Brownell Orwell and Secker & Warburg Ltd.; O'Sullivan, M., *Twenty Years A-Growing*, the author and Chatto & Windus; Porter, K. A., *Flowering Judas*, Jonathan Cape Ltd.; Pritchett, V. S., *Midnight Oil, A Cab at the Door*, A. D. Peters & Co. Ltd.; Pym, B., *No Fond Return of Love, Some Tame Gazelle*, Jonathan Cape Ltd.; Renault, M., *The Last of the Wine*, Penguin Books Ltd.; Russell, B., *The Autobiography*, Allen & Unwin Publishers Ltd.; Sackville-West, V., *The Edwardians*, Michael Joseph; Salinger, J. D., *Catcher in the Rye*, Hamish Hamilton; Sayers, D., *Strong Poison*, Victor Gollancz Ltd.; Sellar & Yeatman, *1066 and All That*, Methuen; Smith, M. C., *Gorky Park*, Collins; Smith, S., *Novel On Yellow Paper*, Jonathan Cape Ltd.; Somerville & Ross, *Dan Russell The Fox*, Methuen; Stephens, J., *The Threepenny Piece, The Blind Man, Three Women, Three Heavy Husbands, The Triangle, Here are Ladies, There is a Tavern in the Town*, The Society of Authors on behalf of the copyright owner, Mrs. Iris Wise; Thompson, E., *The Magic Roundabout*, St. James's Management; Thurber, J., *My Life and Other Times*, Penguin Books Ltd.; Walpole, H., *Portrait of a Man with Red Hair*, Rupert Hart-Davis; Waugh, E., *Decline and Fall, Vile Bodies, Brideshead Revisited*, Chapman & Hall Ltd.; Welch, O., *Mirabeau*, the author and Jonathan Cape Ltd.; Wells, H. G., *Chapter The First, The History of Mr. Polly*, Nelson & Sons Ltd.; White, P., *The Living and the Dead, The Solid Mandala, The Burnt Ones, Riders in the Chariot*, Curtis Brown (Aust) Pty. Ltd.; Wodehouse, P. G., *Blandings Castle, Boxing Final, Some Thoughts on Humourists Over Seventy*, Herbert Jenkins & Penguin Ltd.; Woodham-Smith, C., *The Great Hunger*, Hamish Hamilton Ltd.; Woolf, V., *Jacob's Room, The Voyage Out, Orlando*, the estate of Virginia Woolf and The Hogarth Press; Yeats, W. B., *Magic, Ideas of Good and Evil*, Michael B. Yeats and Macmillan London, Ltd.

INDEX OF AUTHORS